BluesSaxophone

An In-Depth Look at the Styles of the Masters

by Dennis Taylor

CD INCLUDED

Jimmy Forrest and Lester Young photos courtesy of Frank Driggs Collection

Stanley Turrentine photo by Paul Nankin

Illinois Jacquet © 1950 Popsie Randolph/Frank Driggs Collection

Bobby Forte © 1964 Raeburn Flerlage/Frank Driggs Collection

ISBN 0-634-02620-8

HAL•LEONARD®
CORPORATION
7777 W. BLUEMOUND RD. P.O. BOX 13819 MILWAUKEE, WI 53213

www.halleonard.com

PREFACE

In writing this book, I hope to demonstrate the many different approaches possible to playing the blues on the saxophone. By selecting what I consider some of the finest blues players, each with his own unique style, I hope to show that the blues comes in many varying shades—from the rough-hewn Chicago style of Eddie Shaw and A.C. Reed, to the rhythmic jump blues of Red Prysock and Big Jay McNeeley, to the organ-combo soul/jazz of Stanley Turrentine and Willis "Gator" Jackson, to the bebop-inspired blues of Sonny Stitt and Sonny Rollins. The musical possibilities are endless, limited only by your imagination and skill.

Blues plays an integral part in jazz as well as rock and R&B. In every period of jazz development, from swing to bebop to modal, Blues was at the root of the new musical style. Blues is about feel—free-dom—the ability to be more expressive within the less-complicated framework of the chord changes.

"In my time as an A&R man…there were some dates with a lot of paper. And there were times when the players got stuck, as on flypaper…When the music got tangled in the scores, I would leave the control room and would suggest…that maybe they might play some blues. The paper jam broke, and that passe 'blowing session' lasted quite a while to the evident pleasure and relief of the players."

—Nat Hentoff/*JazzTimes*

I've quoted some these players' favorite licks as a launching point. What you are getting is my interpretation of the masters' licks. On the recording, I've played the solos in the style of each player, but obviously could not capture each one's individual tonal characteristics. The saxophone is the closest instrument to the human voice. What I've tried to capture is the "essence" of each person's style.

Please note: The sax tracks on the companion CD can be removed by turning the balance knob all the way to the left, allowing you to play the written solo (or your own) with the band.

I strongly encourage everyone to pick up recordings of each of these artists and listen to them first-hand. To that end, I've included a selected discography for each of the players at the end of each chapter. Learning licks from other players is a building block in learning to improvise; true improvisation is what takes place between the licks. Every solo tells a story. Mastering the solos in this book will help you to improvise in a wide variety of blues styles. Hopefully, you'll also come to invent your own licks. The ultimate goal, of course, is to have one's own distinct voice. It's the unique combination of all of the influences and the individual tone quality that sets each of these artists apart. Stravinsky once said something to the effect that, "A lesser artist borrows; a great artist steals." Feel free to "steal" some of these licks and make them your own.

—Dennis Taylor

TABLE OF CONTENTS

Photo © Ray Flerlage/Frank Driggs Collection

Eddie Shaw looking cool in the studio,
blowing a bluesy solo on his King Super 20 saxophone.

EDDIE SHAW

(1937 –)

When it comes to blues, Chicago is primarily a guitar and harmonica town. One of the few exceptions to that rule is renowned Chicago blues saxophonist Eddie Shaw. In a career that has spanned over forty years, Shaw has played with many of the Chicago's legendary bluesmen, including Howlin' Wolf, Muddy Waters, Magic Sam, Otis Rush, Willie Dixon, Freddy King, Hound Dog Taylor, and Earl Hooker.

As a teenager growing up in Greenville, MS, Eddie Shaw backed up R&B greats Little Milton and Ike Turner. Equally adept at playing swing and blues, Shaw was hired by Muddy Waters after sitting in with his band in 1958. Shaw moved to Chicago at Muddy's request. One night at a gig, Shaw had an argument with fellow band members over the sloppiness of the band's performance and quit the gig before Muddy arrived that night. He packed up his horn, walked five blocks down the street, and sat in with Muddy's chief rival, Howlin' Wolf. Wolf immediately hired him, and that began a nearly twenty-year alliance. Shaw became Wolf's right-hand man, eventually performing the duties of bandleader, arranger, and road manager.

Shaw's reputation as a sideman continued to grow with his stellar performances on Wolf's '65–'67 Chess recordings and Magic Sam's 1968 release *Black Magic* (Delmark). Shaw's own recording career began taking off after Wolf's death in 1976. With a scintillating performance on Alligator Records' *Living Chicago Blues* anthology released in 1978, Shaw's solo career gained momentum. Eddie Shaw continues to tour and record with his own band, Eddie Shaw and the Wolf Gang.

Musically Speaking:

"I think playing the horn like I do is something like the old Baptist preacher. When a Baptist preacher preaches in church, everybody listens. He shouts out what he wants you to hear, and he brings it to you in such a way that you're gonna listen. So that's the same way I try to do it with the saxophone. I try to have a good attack, don't try to play a lot of notes, try to stay with the basics and tell a good story."

As told to Bill Dahl, *Chicago Tribune*, Sunday 9/20/92.

The following is an example of a standard 12-bar Chicago blues shuffle with a traditional V–IV turnaround instead of the jazzier ii–V7 turnaround. Eddie Shaw likes to play on the front side of the beat to create rhythmic tension, as opposed to the laid-back style of someone like Gene Ammons or Maxwell Davis (to be discussed later). Using a composite blues scale that features a minor 3rd and a major 3rd (A–C–C♯–D–E♭–E♮–G), nearly every C♯ is preceded by a C♮. Shaw has a penchant for using the A minor pentatonic scale (A–C–D–E–G) on the IV chords. This creates an implied sus4 chord sound due to the third of the chord (F♯) being omitted.

At measure C10, a chromatic run up the scale starting on the major 7 of the D7 chord builds tension leading into the last chorus. Section D is a standard riff that can be incorporated into your improvisation or used as a background riff behind someone else's solo.

Fig. 1

Eddie Shaw Selected Discography

1968   Magic Sam/*Black Magic* – Delmark

1978   Various artists/*Living Chicago Blues Vol. 1* – Alligator

1985   *King Of The Road* – Rooster Blues

1992   *In The Land Of The Crossroads* – Rooster Blues

1994   Howlin' Wolf/*Ain't Gonna Be Your Dog* – MCA/Original Chess Masters

Photo by James Fraher

A.C. Reed clowning with the audience at the Chicago Blues Festival in 1989.
Notice his electric sax setup with a condenser mic attached to the neck of his horn.

A.C. REED

(1926 –)

In the world of Chicago blues dominated by guitarists and harp players, A.C. (Aaron Corthen) Reed has been a much sought-after sideman. A.C. was inspired to play sax upon hearing Paul Bascomb's sax solo on Erskine Hawkins' "Beer-Mash Blues" in 1942. Born in Wardell, MO, Reed moved to Chicago in the early forties and bought his first sax. He went to the Chicago Music Conservatory to learn the fundamentals—specifically how to read music—so he could play big-band swing (which he never got to pursue).

Reed got his start playing around Chicago with blues guitarist Earl Hooker. In 1948, he joined pianist Willie Mabon's band. During this time, he met fellow Elmore James' sax player J.T. Brown, who coached him in the ins and outs of playing blues. In 1956, Reed joined ex-Ike Turner bassist Dennis "Long Man" Binder's band, touring the Southwest from their home base in Oklahoma. In the early sixties, Reed moved back to Chicago and reunited with Hooker. Together they played sessions for producer Mel London's Age and Chief labels. During the sixties, Reed recorded as a vocalist for small local Chicago labels like USA, Nike, and Cool. In 1967, he joined Buddy Guy's band and soon found himself playing for white college kids and traveling around the world. (In 1970, the band was the Rolling Stones' opening act.) In 1977 Reed joined Son Seals' band, and in 1978 he was recruited by Albert Collins, with whom he stayed for five years, playing on Collins' first five Alligator Records releases. While playing with Collins, he developed an international reputation. That, coupled with 1980's *Living Chicago Blues Vol. 3* album (which featured him on four cuts), helped Reed's solo career to take off. His 1982 solo debut album on the small Ice Cube label (co-founded with Albert Collins' drummer Casey Jones) was called *Take These Blues and Shove 'Em!* (re-released later by Rooster Blues). Five years later, he released *I'm In The Wrong Business!* for Alligator Records. This acclaimed release featured guest stars Bonnie Raitt and Stevie Ray Vaughan. Reed, with his band the Spark Plugs, continues to blow his tough urban blues around the Windy City.

Musically speaking:

Modern electric Chicago blues ace saxman A.C. Reed, with his tough, gritty tone and tongue-in-cheek lyrics, was influenced by Paul Bascomb and fellow Chicago tenor player Gene Ammons. Reed's role in Chicago blues bands has been much the same as the role of the harp player—running counterpoint and counter rhythms to the guitarist and filling in between the vocals.

This example of A.C. Reed's style is primarily based on the B minor pentatonic scale (B–D–E–F♯–A). The only time he deviates from that scale is in measure A5, where he plays a C♯ (the 5th of the F♯7) and in measures B5 and B6, where he hits the same C♯, this time functioning as the 6th of the E7 chord. Hitting those C♯s adds contrast and color, giving the dark minor tonality a brief "lift." The rest of the solo is based on five notes, but Reed gets lots of mileage from them by his deft use of rhythm.

Fig. 2

A.C. Reed Selected Discography

1978   Albert Collins/*Ice Pickin'* – Alligator

1981   Earl Hooker/*Blue Guitar* – Paula/Flyrite

1982   *Take These Blues and Shove 'Em!* – Rooster Blues

1987   *I'm In The Wrong Business!* – Alligator

Frank Driggs Collection

*Maxwell Davis, one of the architects of the West Coast R&B sound,
playing in Los Angeles in 1944.*

MAXWELL DAVIS

(1916 – 1970)

Maxwell Davis was one of the architects of the West Coast R&B sound. During the late forties and into the fifties, he had a large impact on the musical scene through his numerous roles as a saxophonist, bandleader, songwriter, arranger, producer, and A&R man (mainly working for the Modern and Aladdin record labels).

Raised in Kansas, by the time Maxwell Davis was a teenager he had discovered jazz and was deeply influenced by Coleman Hawkins. In 1937, he moved to Los Angeles and landed a gig with the Fletcher Henderson Orchestra. Soon afterwards, he found work arranging songs and producing sessions for B.B. King, T-Bone Walker, Clarence "Gatemouth" Brown, Z.Z. Hill, Johnny "Guitar" Watson, and Lowell Fulson. Combining his love of jazz and blues, he created a formula that utilized a swinging rhythm section and a big band-style horn section to backup a strong blues-based frontman, usually a guitar player. His influence was soon heard in the music of Percy Mayfield, Jimmy Witherspoon, and Floyd Dixon.

Maxwell Davis penned "Bad, Bad, Whisky," one of boogie-woogie piano player Amos Milburn's biggest hits. Davis released dozens of song titles under his own name, but only the song "Slow Walk" met with any success. With the rise of self-contained rock & roll bands in the sixties, Davis faded from the musical scene.

Musically speaking:

Maxwell Davis had a big, warm, smoky sound. Influenced by Coleman Hawkins and Ben Webster, his blues/West Coast R&B was infused with swing.

Here is a medium-tempo West Coast blues in the style of guitarist T-Bone Walker. Very relaxed in style, Davis' phrasing is constantly behind the beat. The entire first chorus is built from the motif of the first three notes. Measures A1, A2, A6, A8, and A10 are all developed from the same three-note intro. A chromatic run leads us into the second chorus, which is mainly played on the G minor pentatonic scale (G–B♭–C–D♭–F). This is a good example of taking a simple idea and expanding upon it ("telling a story"). The solo comes to a climax in the middle of the second chorus, then winds back down. Notice how the first chorus has a major sound and the second chorus is more minor or bluesy. This contrast helps build the solo and give the listener the sense of the soloist digging in.

Fig. 3

Maxwell Davis Selected Discography

1991   *T-Bone Walker: The Complete Imperial Recordings, 1950-1954* – EMI/Imperial

1993   *The Best of Amos Milburn: Down The Road Apiece* – EMI/Aladdin

*Bobby Forte (right) with B.B. King and his band
at the Regal Theater in Chicago, 1964.*

BOBBY FORTE

(1943 – 2000)

Often overlooked, lifelong sideman Bobby Forte was one of the most soulful tenor players of his era. Born Bobby Hunt in Paris, TX, Forte moved to Oakland, CA at the age of twelve. His mother was gospel singer Dorothy Hunt, and her gospel singing had a profound impact on Forte's playing style throughout his life. At the age of fifteen, he left home and joined Bobby "Blue" Bland's band and played on many of his biggest hits, including "Cry, Cry, Cry," "I Pity The Fool," and a featured obbligato on "Turn On Your Love Lights." Forte joined B. B. King's band in 1964, and he appears on such albums as *Blues Is King, Lucille, Live At The Regal, Guess Who,* and the B.B. King/Bobby "Blue" Bland collaboration *Together For The First Time.* Bobby Forte also recorded with Buddy Ace, Lowell Fulson, his mother Dorothy Hunt, Percy Mayfield, Charles Brown, Jimmy McCracklin, and Charlie Musselwhite, among others.

Musically Speaking:

Strongly influenced by Gene Ammons and "Fathead" Newman, Bobby Forte had a thick, passionate sound with deep gospel roots.

This solo is based on two eight-bar choruses. Nearly all the notes come from the F# major pentatonic scale (F#–G#–A#–C#–D#). To achieve that authentic sanctified soul approach, Forte relied on playing a lot of major 6ths, 3rds, and 9ths (as in measures A1, A2, A3, and A6), coloring the chords F#7, C#, and B7. In measure A11, a flat 5 (C♮) is quickly played in passing, resolving to a B on the F# chord and accenting the flat 7 on the B chord. In the beginning of the second chorus, the first four bars are back to a major tonality followed by the contrast of the "blue notes" in the last four bars to give it a mournful, soul sound. There's a good example of the bebop Mixolydian scale in measure B6.

Fig. 4

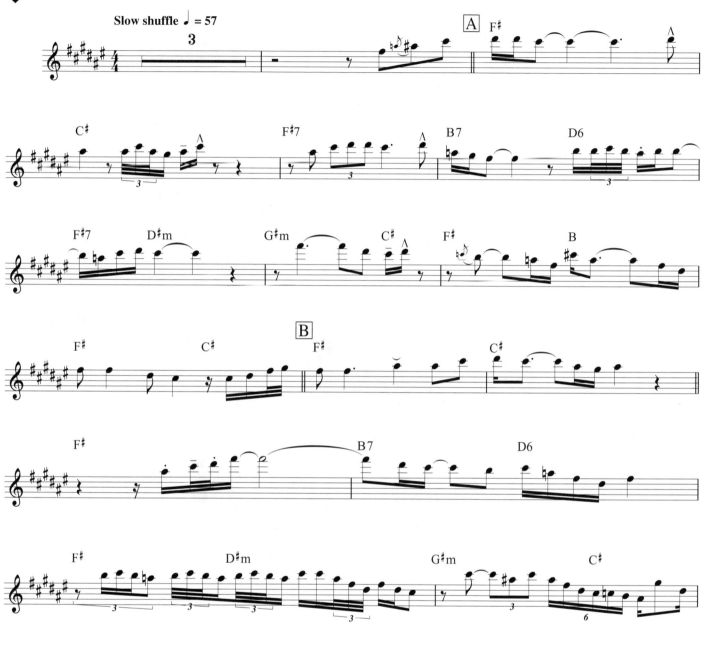

Bobby Forte Selected Discography

1960-64   Bobby "Blue" Bland/
           Turn On Your Love Lights: The Duke Recordings, Vols. 1 & 2 – Duke

1965   B.B. King/*Live At The Regal* – MCA

1967   B.B. King/*Blues Is King* – MCA

1992   Charles Brown/*Someone To Love* – Rounder

Frank Driggs Collection

*Lee Allen holds down the piano for Little Richard while
blowing a hot New Orleans R&B solo in 1957.*

LEE ALLEN

(1926 – 1994)

Lee Allen was one of the few purveyors of New Orleans R&B who was not a native. Raised in Denver, CO, he arrived in New Orleans on an athletic scholarship to Xavier University in 1944. He left school before graduating to join Paul Gayten's band. During this same period, Allen became a fixture at Cosimo Matassa's J & M Studios as a member of the famed studio band. Through this opportunity, he developed a saxophone style that would help define the role of sax in New Orleans R&B and early Rock 'n' Roll.

Allen plays on such classics as Fats Domino's "I'm Walking," Little Richard's "Tutti Frutti," Shirley and Lee's "Let The Good Times Roll," and Huey "Piano" Smith's "Don't You Just Know It." In 1956, he stepped out on his own and recorded "Shimmy" and "Rockin' at Cosimo's" for Aladdin Records. (Neither song did much.) His follow-up single, "Walkin' with Mr. Lee" (Ember), was a modest hit, spending eleven weeks on the Billboard charts. He toured fronting his own band for the next few years, until hooking up with Fats Domino in 1961. He stayed with Fats until 1965 when he moved to Los Angeles.

Throughout the seventies, gigs were hard to come by, and Allen took a job in the aeronautics industry, but still joined Fats on tour from time to time. In the early eighties, a few rockabilly bands, including the Stray Cats and the Blasters, called on Allen to play. (Allen met Dave Alvin when Alvin contacted him about taking sax lessons.) One of his final sessions was the *Crescent City Gold* album, on which he reunited with many of his old J&M Studio colleagues to record new versions of New Orleans classics. Allen died in Los Angeles in October 1994.

Musically Speaking:

Allen's style incorporates the rhythmic sense of Lester Young and the muscular arpeggiated approach of Coleman Hawkins. "I really copied my tone around Coleman Hawkins. I always loved his sound." Other influences include Illinois Jacquet, Gene Ammons, and Louis Jordan. Allen possessed a full, round tone; his playing was earthy, ebullient, and joyous. He had a strong and simple melodic approach and innately knew what was appropriate for each song. His solos became as much a part of the song structure as the chord progression and lyrics. "I didn't try to play differently behind each individual; I played the way I felt. I got my message from the singer and stayed close to the melody line of the song." He prided himself on never being a "honker."

Here is an excellent example of Lee Allen's lyrical style—a 12-bar New Orleans shuffle (a sound quite prevalent in R&B records of the late fifties). Notice how Allen never ventures far from the melody; it's as if he was just singing through his horn. Basically playing an F blues scale throughout, he makes nice use of the flat 5 in measures C3, C5, and C6, and E6-8. The note choices are simple and basic; it's his use of rhythm that makes him unique. He gets such a nice lope in his stride that he puts his listener completely at ease. Notice the way he develops measures D5–12, taking a simple rhythm and twisting and turning it around, building tension until it comes full circle back to the original rhythm and release at letter E. The climax of the solo begins at measure E7 using a short repeated figure off the flat 5, then repeated notes and rhythm to propel the solo to its conclusion (measures E8–11).

Fig. 5

Lee Allen Selected Discography

1958   *Walkin' with Mr. Lee* – Collectables

1972   *Dr. John's Gumbo* - Alligator

1991   *They Call Me The Fat Man…The Legendary Imperial Recordings* – EMI America

Photo by Doug DuKane

Seventy-six year old Noble Watts, still active playing his brand of "Southern-fried" soul.

NOBLE "THIN MAN" WATTS

(1926 –)

Born in Deland, Florida, Noble Watts' first instrument was the piano. He tried violin and trumpet before settling on the sax. In 1942, he enrolled in Florida A&M, where he played in the marching band with the Adderly Brothers, Cannonball and Nat. After college, he joined the Griffin Brothers touring R&B band. In 1952, he teamed with Paul "Hucklebuck" Williams and recorded with him for the Jax label. He also worked with Dinah Washington, Amos Milburn, and Ruth Brown, and had a short stay with vibraphonist Lionel Hampton.

In 1956, now out on his own, Watts had an instrumental dance hit with the song "The Slop" on the Baton label (the label's first Top 40 hit). A radio station, uncomfortable with airing a tune with that title, persuaded the record company to rename the tune "Hard Times."

Watts stayed with the Baton label until 1959. During the fifties he played on many rock 'n' roll package tours, backing Jerry Lee Lewis, Buddy Holly, Chuck Berry, The Everly Brothers, Fats Domino, The Coasters, and The Drifters.

At the peak of his popularity in the fifties and early sixties, Watts was managed by boxer Sugar Ray Robinson, who employed him as the leader of the house band in his club in Harlem, NY. Hard times found Watts in the sixties when the sax fell out of favor with pop music. In the early seventies he was a member of the house band at the famed Apollo Theater. Watts split his home base between NY and Florida before finally moving back to his hometown of Deland in 1983. Kingsnake Records producer Bob Greenlee heard Watts playing at a party and convinced him to record for his new label. The result was 1987's *Return Of The Thin Man*, with special guest Taj Mahal.

Musically Speaking:

Noble "Thin Man" Watts' distinctive "greasy-voiced" and funky soul/gospel "Southern fried" saxophone has elements of jump-blues as well as King Curtis- and Junior Walker-style R&B.

This example of Southern soul is languidly phrased throughout with notes played lazily behind the beat. In the A section, the notes are all part of the F♯ major pentatonic scale (F♯–G♯–A♯–C♯–D♯) with the exception of measures B5-6. The F♯ trill in measures A4 and A12 is played by fingering F♯ and trilling the G finger. The B section is a little bluesier, with the use of a hybrid scale combining a blues scale and a Mixolydian (F♯–G♯–A–A♯–B–C–C♯–E). This scale is widely used by everyone from B.B. King to Charlie Parker and is one you should know and be able to use.

6 Fig. 6

Noble "Thin Man" Watts Selected Discography

1987   *Return of the Thin Man* – Kingsnake/Alligator

1993   *King of the Boogie Sax* – Wild Dog/Ichiban

An early publicity photo of King Curtis,
one of the most influential R&B saxophonists.

KING CURTIS

(1934 – 1971)

One of the last of the great R&B tenor saxophonists, King Curtis was born Curtis Ousley in Fort Worth, Texas. The son of a guitar player, Curtis got his first sax—an alto—at age twelve, and switched to tenor in high school. By the time he was thirteen, he was gigging around Fort Worth, and two years later he had his own R&B band. After graduating high school, he visited his uncle in New York City—the trip convinced Curtis that New York was the place to be. He moved to NYC in the early fifties and quickly came to prominence as a session player.

If it was an R&B session in NY from the mid-fifties through the sixties, it was most likely King Curtis on saxophone. He's featured on The Coasters' "Yakety Yak," Bobby Darin's "Splish Splash," Ben E. King's "Spanish Harlem," and recordings by Sam Cooke, the Drifters, and the Shirelles. He played on countless recordings with artists as diverse as Buddy Holly, Andy Williams, and John Lennon. His long association with Atlantic/Atco began in 1958. Curtis also played on some of Aretha's finest recordings, including the famous sax solo on "Respect."

After making a name for himself as a session musician, Curtis struck out on his own. He had a #1 R&B single with his funky instrumental "Soul Twist" (Enjoy Records) in 1962. He signed briefly with Capitol Records, but they didn't really know what to do with him. In 1965, he signed with Atlantic/Atco, beginning a long and successful relationship. Curtis had hits with his songs "Memphis Soul Stew" and his instrumental version of "Ode To Billie Joe" (from his 1967 *King Size Soul* album). In the sixties, Curtis electrified his sound using a wah-wah pedal. It fit the sound of the times and certainly made him stand out from the rest of the pack. Curtis' band, first called the Noble Knights and then the Kingpins, featured the all-star lineup of Richard Tee (piano), Cornell Dupree (guitar), Bernard Purdie (drums), Jerry Jemmott (bass), and sometimes Billy Preston on organ. This group also backed Aretha on various sessions as well as live performances. One of these performances resulted in the dual live recordings called *Live At The Fillmore*. King Curtis was murdered outside his NYC apartment in August 1971.

Musically speaking:

King Curtis began as a jazz player influenced by Gene Ammons as well as Louis Jordan, Arnett Cobb, and Lester Young. His tough Texas tenor, with its flowing jazz lines, evolved into a rapid-fire staccato approach largely to accommodate the guitar-driven funkier rhythm sections of commercial R&B.

This solo is a classic example of funky Southern soul. It begins with a twelve-measure vamp intro in the key of F♯, which then serves as the V chord when the song modulates to the new key of B (Section A). The opening lick is one of King Curtis' most identifiable ones, based on a guitar picking style called "chicken pickin'." This staccato way of phrasing was the basis of Curtis' solo on The Coasters' hit "Yakey Yak" and was later adopted by Boots Randolph for "Yakety Sax." The flutter-tonguing technique at the seventh and eighth measure of the intro is achieved by rolling your tongue like you are rolling your rrrs. The rest of the solo is based on the B major pentatonic scale and demonstrates Curtis' crisp staccato tonguing punctuated by high squeals—a style that was to cross musical genres from R&B into pop and rock 'n' roll.

Fig. 7

King Curtis Selected Discography

1960-64   *Soul Twist* – Collectables

1962   *Soul Meeting* – Prestige

1967   *King Size Soul* – Collectables

Big Jay McNeely "jumping" the blues.

BIG JAY MCNEELY

(1927 –)

The mighty titan of the tenor sax, Big Jay McNeely's paint-peeling squealing and honking made him the torch bearer of the R&B and early rock 'n' roll scene of the fifties and sixties. Born Cecil McNeely and raised in the Watts section of Los Angeles, he and his brother Bob shared time on the family's only saxophone. Inspired by Illinois Jacquet and Jack McVea, the young Cecil became a fixture on L.A.'s Central Avenue. A friend of Johnny Otis' heard McNeely and produced his first recording for Savoy in 1948. Savoy boss Herman Lubinsky changed Cecil's name to Big Jay, thinking it would be more commercial-sounding.

Big Jay McNeely had his first hit in 1949 with "Deacon's Hop." He quickly became known for his ability to blow torrid solos from every conceivable position—on his knees, on his back, while strolling through the audience...he put the "hip" in showmanship. In 1949, at a show at a baseball park in Los Angeles, McNeely blew his sax through the stands, down onto the field going from home plate to first base, crawling on his back! He also would perform wearing white gloves and playing a fluorescent painted saxophone lit by black lights for a glow-in-the-dark effect.

Throughout the early fifties, McNeely continued to record for the Exclusive, Imperial, and King's Federal subsidiary labels. At the same time, his live shows had become legendary. In 1959, he landed back on the charts, this time with the bluesy number "There is Something on Your Mind," sung by Little Sonny Warner. With the advent of soul music and the British Invasion in the sixties, honking saxophonists fell out of favor. McNeely curtailed his touring and took a job at the post office. But by the eighties, Europe's fascination with early R&B heroes had drawn McNeely back onto the scene. He was invited to perform for the Grammy Awards in 1987, sharing the stage with Etta James, Koko Taylor, Willie Dixon, B.B. King, Albert King, Dr. John, Junior Wells, and Robert Cray. He now splits his time living in Europe and the States, keeping a fairly active touring and recording schedule.

Musically speaking:

Big Jay McNeely always played the entire range of the horn. From the high squeals to the low honks, his unique style was readily identifiable.

This McNeely-style solo opens with a classic jump-style blues riff. Section B demonstrates his low-note honking and repeated note riffing that were a staples of this genre of sax playing in the late forties and through the fifties. McNeely doesn't often use the blues scale in his playing, but in measure C2 the B♭ blues scale is used, leading to the high F in measure C3 to add harmonic color. In measures C11 and C12, chromaticism is used to build excitement leading into the fourth chorus. Measures D5 through D12 feature one of McNeely's pet licks—repeating the B-flats and using octave displacement, ultimately building tension in measure D10 by hitting the low B-natural and finally resolving to the low B-flat. Section E features the high screams on altissimo D and F, followed by the fall all the way back down the the low B-flat—these are essential elements of McNeely's style. The trills at measures F9 and F10 are played by using the regular fingering and trilling with the top side key in the right hand.

Try playing this entire solo without the octave key, for two reasons: it will help strengthen and firm up your embouchere, and it will also help you achieve a more authentic tone for this style of R&B playing.

Fig. 8

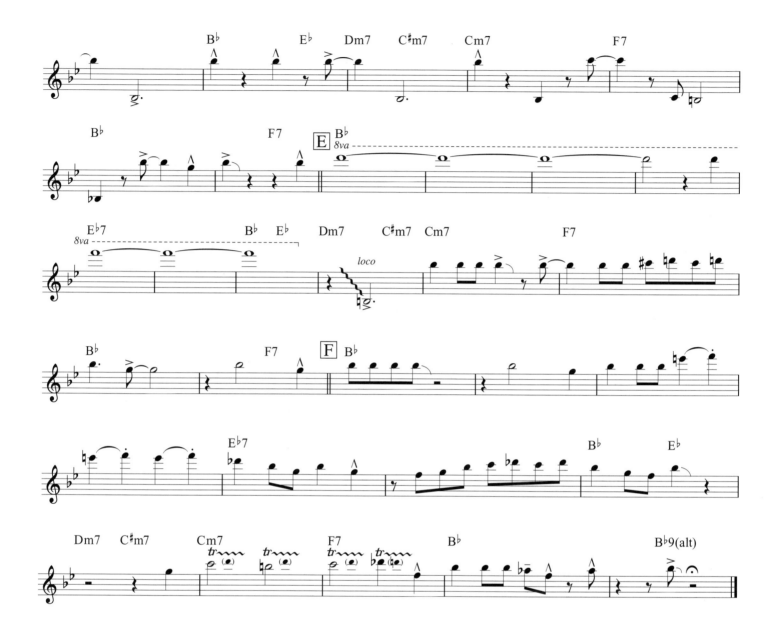

Big Jay McNeely Selected Discography

Red Prysock, one of the first R&B saxophonists, blowing one of his blazing solos.

WILBERT "RED" PRYSOCK

(1926 – 1993)

"Red" Prysock's jump-based blues solos were the cornerstone of rock 'n' roll. Wilbert Prysock grew up in Greensboro, North Carolina. After trying his hand at piano, organ, clarinet, and trumpet, he settled on saxophone after his sister bought him a sax for his seventeenth birthday. He was drafted in 1944, and while in the service he applied himself to playing the sax.

By the time of his discharge in 1947, Prysock was good enough to get a gig with guitarist Tiny Grimes, who had just signed to the fledgling Atlantic Records label. Red had so much power and excitement in his playing, a lot of Grimes' material was structured to showcase him. Grimes'ensemble had a hit called "Loch Lomond," and they changed their name to the Rockin' Highlanders and performed in kilts—that was enough to make Red move on. Shortly after that, Red joined Tiny Bradshaw's band. In the early fifties, Bradshaw got a big break when his band recorded "Soft," which became an R&B smash hit. Red was featured on the tune and started to make his reputation. In 1953, Red joined Cootie Williams' band for a brief stay, then in 1954 recorded his first two jump-blues singles for Mercury Records—"Jump, Red, Jump" and "Blow Your Horn." Heavily influenced by Illinois Jacquet, Red was the king of the one-note solos, often repeating one note for a number of choruses. He gained tremendous exposure after landing the gig on Alan Freed's Rock 'n' Roll Jubilee Ball in NYC in 1955. That led to working on other Rock 'n' Roll package tours. With the advent of soul music in the sixties, Red, able to adapt his style, played on numerous sessions for both the King and Chess labels. In 1971, he teamed up with his older brother, vocalist Arthur Prysock, playing a smoother jazz style.

Musically speaking:

More than a honker and screamer, Red Prysock demonstrated a greater musical depth than most of his contemporaries. Red had great feel and blazing technique, featuring a robust tone and, at times, almost a bebop phrasing.

This example of Red Prysock's jump-blues style is based on a 32-measure AABA song form. It begins with a sixteen-measure intro with only a closed hi-hat for accompaniment. Using the overtone fingering to change the timbre of the repeated C's (a device first pioneered by Lester Young) creates the desired percussive effect. The bridge is a I–IV–II–V progression and is commonly referred to as a "Flying Home" bridge. The solo is very linear in nature and calls upon the use of chromaticism (measures A6, A13, and A14) and blues-scale licks (in measures A7 and A11, for example). On the bridges, Red would usually start very inside for the first two measures of the I7 chord, mainly hitting chord tones, but would move to upper extension alterations on the IV7, II7, and V7 chords, sounding $\sharp$9s and $\flat$9s to provide a jazzier tonality. At measure A27, the B$\flat$ is played by fingering E$\flat$ and lifting up the G finger.

It's important to keep the larynx flexible and move it into a position to make that "shake" like a trumpet player. It wouldn't be "authentic" jump blues without certain dramatic devices, such as utilizing the entire range of the horn, the repeated rhythms at section B, the sixteen bars at section C, the high squeal at measure C17, and the low honks at section D coupled with overtone fingerings. Red's jump-blues approach is actually much more complex than one would assume from first listen.

9 Fig. 9

Wilbert "Red" Prysock Selected Discography

1996   *Rock On Roll - The Best of Red Prysock* – AVI/Polygram

1959   *Battle Royal! (w/Sil Austin)* – Mercury

*Illinois Jacquet playing one of his crowd-pleasing solos with the
Lionel Hampton Orchestra at Carnegie Hall in 1950.*

ILLINOIS JACQUET

(1922 –)

An important, often-overlooked transitional figure in the development of tenor saxophone, Illinois Jacquet made significant contributions to jazz while remaining true to his Texas blues roots. He was the bridge between swing and jump blues.

Illinois Jacquet was born Jean Baptiste Illinois Jacquet in Boussard, Louisiana in 1922. He was raised in Houston, Texas and grew up in a showbiz family. He and his three older brothers were a tap dance team for their multi-instrumentalist father Gilbert's orchestra, and Illinois was on stage for the first time at age three. Under the tutelege of his father, Jacquet began as a drummer, but switched to saxophone by the time he was in grade school. In high school, he joined Houston bandleader Milt Larkin, playing alto in a sax section that included Arnett Cobb and Eddie "Cleanhead" Vinson. They toured the South with their bluesy swing sound.

Upon graduation, Jacquet move to LA and got noticed at a jam session by Nat Cole. Cole recommended him to Lionel Hampton, who was forming his own big band. Hamp asked Jacquet to switch to tenor. Jacquet got to hone his skills with steady work and exposure on a national level; he played with the band for two years (1941-43). Jacquet's incredible 64-bar solo on the tune "Flying Home" (recorded with Hampton's band on May 26, 1942) became an integral part of the song—everyone who played that song afterwards had to play his solo. The impact of that solo actually helped to popularize the sax.

In 1943, Jacquet left Hampton to join Cab Calloway's band, with whom he worked for the next two years. His 1944 appearance in Norman Granz' first "Jazz at the Philharmonic" Concert provided him with another showcase opportunity. The concert was recorded, and Jacquet's screaming solo on "Blues Part II" caused an uproar—he brought to crowd to its feet with his wailing altissimo notes and percussive low honks. Few could match his competitive fury. It was during these JATP jams that Jacquet earned his nickname "the Beast" because of his take-no-prisoners approach. He joined the band of his childhood idol, Count Basie, from 1945-46.

In 1948, Jacquet moved to New York City and formed his own band, recording juke box hits including "Port of Rico" and "Lean Baby" for Cleff Records. That same year, he appeared on Ed Sullivan's TV show "Toast of the Town," becoming the first jazz musician to appear on national television. During the fifties and sixties he continued to lead his own band, recording steadily playing swing and bop. In the early eighties he received an invitation from Harvard University to lecture and play for their jazz history course. Inspired by this experience, he formed his own big band in 1983—his first in nearly thirty years. He's still active today.

Musically speaking:

Illinois Jacquet defined the Texas tenor school. More than just a honker, he also possessed the finesse to give lush renderings to ballads and slow blues numbers. Jacquet's playing featured a round tone with an aggressive attack. Always self-assured, he was a powerful soloist fueled by his amazing technique; he knew how to play to a crowd. You could hear the blues in everything he played. Influenced by the Count Basie Orchestra saxophone tradition, he was a combination of Herschel Evans and Lester Young.

Jacquet became the inspiration for an entire generation of soul, jazz, and R&B tenor sax players. He influenced Joe Houston, Red Prysock, Eddie "Lockjaw" Davis, and Big Jay McNeely, to name a few.

This example is based on a 32-measure AABA song form. It incorporates Jacquet's swing style with his flair for the dramatic. From section A to B, it is pure swing in the Coleman Hawkins/Herschel Evans tradition, running arpeggios to outline the chord progression. At section B, the eighth-note pulse is gone, and we dig into the blues by playing longer notes emphasizing the root and 3rd. At measure B9, the solo builds up to the modulation by stretching the time with half notes for eight measures. Section A was swing; section B is jump blues. At the four-bar break, the change of key is negotiated by playing the first measure-and-a-half in B♭, then hitting a B♭ augmented triad followed by a C augmented triad, landing on the low B♭ which serves as the five in the new key (E♭). Section C swings out on a riff à la Count Basie.

10 **Fig. 10**

Illinois Jacquet Selected Discography

1961   *The Blues That's Me* – Prestige

1962   *Flying Home* – RCA Bluebird

1969   *Soul Explosion* – Prestige

1988   *Jacquet's Got It: Illinois Jacquet and his Big Band* – Atlantic

1993   *Illinois Jacquet Flying Home: The Best of the Verve Years* – Verve

Striking his trademark side-arm stance, "Prez" Lester Young steps out front of the Count Basie Orchestra at the Treasure Island Music Hall in San Francisco, 1939.

LESTER YOUNG

(1909 – 1959)

Lester Young was born in Mississippi and raised in Algiers, Louisiana, across the river from New Orleans. He was taught drums, trumpet, alto sax, and violin by his bandleading father and spent most of his youth playing drums in the Young family band. By his late teens, he had quit the family band, given up the drums, and switched to alto sax. (He noticed that all the young women had left the gig by the time he finished packing up his drum kit.)

Young joined Art Bronson's Bostonians as a tenor sax player from 1928-29. After the Bronson band, he freelanced for a few years with Bennie Moten, King Oliver, and had a brief stint with the Count Basie Orchestra. In 1934, he joined Fletcher Henderson's Orchestra, filling Coleman Hawkins' vacated chair. Young's light, airy tone and linear approach was too foreign to Henderson's sidemen and was met with great opposition. Henderson's wife would take Young into their basement and make him study Hawkins' recorded solos to learn how to play "correctly." Although his playing was pleasing to Henderson, the mocking of the other sidemen led Young to leave the band after only a few months. In 1936, he rejoined the Basie Orchestra and was with the band when it relocated to New York City. He made his recording debut that year on the John Hammond-produced four-song session with a small version of Basie's band. The impact of two of those songs, "Lady Be Good" and "Shoe Shine Boy," was revolutionary and challenged Coleman Hawkins' reign as the top sax soloist. Young's mellow sound and hard-swinging solos were a perfect fit with the Basie Orchestra, and soon he was the featured soloist—and a major attraction for the band. For the next four years, he played on all of the Count's recording dates, as well as some of Billie Holliday's finest recordings. His light touch and gravity-free style of playing was a perfect blend with Holliday. She proclaimed him the "President of the Saxophone," which got shortened to "Prez," and he affectionately dubbed her "Lady Day." From 1940-43, "Prez" left the Basie Orchestra and had his own group for a while, co-leading a band with his brother, drummer Lee Young. He also worked with Al Sears' Big Band. In 1943, he returned to the Basie Orchestra, but a recording strike kept the band from making any records during this period. (A few air checks are all that have been preserved.)

Young was drafted in 1944. Shortly after his induction, he was sentenced to a prison term at a detention barracks in Georgia—the charge stemmed from his admission on a routine form that he smoked pot. He was said to have been beaten and abused. His time served left deep scars on his inner psyche, and the youthful exuberance in his playing was gone. In 1945, after being discharged, he resumed recording. The first tune cut was "DB Blues" (DB = Detention Barracks). A more revealing and vulnerable quality had appeared in his playing.

Young made some of his finest recordings during the latter half of the forties and maintained his spot in the hierarchy of jazz soloists despite the advent of bebop. Throughout the fifties, he led his own combo and had a few reunions with Basie. Always a loner, Young grew more retiring and distrusting. His health got progressively worse due to his alcoholism. In March of 1959, he died in his NYC hotel room, just hours after returning from an engagement in Paris.

Musically speaking:

Lester Young was profoundly original—from his dress, to his own invented language, to his way of holding his sax off-center at a rakish angle, to coming into the world of Coleman Hawkins and creating a completely new way of playing. His style was based on lyricism with a deep sense of swing. Young's diaphanous tone and flowing glissandos gave his playing a sense of soaring. He always played from the heart and commanded attention. Young is perhaps the most emulated sax player in the history of jazz, and his importance is second to none.

This slow 12-bar blues serves up an example of Young's linear approach. His long fluid scale runs, negotiating the changes, are the complete antithesis of Coleman Hawkins' vertical approach. Young's phrases often take unexpected twists and turns and are filled with deceptive resolutions (as in measures A6-7, A8-9, B4-5, B8-9, and C3-4). His solos have an ethereal quality due to the combination of his tone and his love of playing the upper entensions of the chord—mainly the 9th and 6th. This became a direct influence on Charlie Parker's style. In the first two choruses, the 3rd of the chord is sounded quickly and only in passing. Not until section C is the 3rd played on a strong beat and for any duration (bar C1). Young had an acute sense of rhythm that he would use to build tension. Playing a Louis Armstrong-like swing riff in measures B1, B3, and B6, the tension is then released with a long descending line (measures B7-8). The third chorus begins by hitting the defining notes of the chord (3rds and 7ths), giving the listener the sense of digging into the changes in contrast to the earlier choruses' feel of floating over the top. The solo then concludes with a sequenced line that spirals downward (measures C7-10) leading into a blues scale lick that retards and resolves into the final chord.

 Fig. 11

Lester Young Selected Discography

1936-39   *Essential Count Basie Vol. 1 & 2* – Columbia Jazz Master

1946   *Complete Lester Young on Keynote* – Verve (w/Nat King Cole & Buddy Rich)

1956   *Lester Young w/The Oscar Peterson Trio* – Verve

1994   *Lester Young Jazz Masters 30 – 1943-1952* – Verve

1997   *The Kansas City Sessions 1938-1944* – GRP

*Gene Ammons' style combined the harmonic sophistication of bebop
with the soulful, gritty edge of the blues.*

GENE "JUG" AMMONS

(1925 – 1974)

Son of boogie-woogie piano player Albert Ammons, Gene Ammons ("Jug") blended R&B, blues, and bebop.

Gene Ammons was raised in Chicago. At the age of eighteen he joined trumpeter King Kolax' blues band. Ammons first came into national prominence when he joined Billy Eckstine's seminal big band (1944-47), in which he was used primarily as the bebop-style soloist. He's featured on the "tenor battle" with Dexter Gordon on Eckstine's record *Blowing The Blues Away*. When Eckstine's band disbanded, Ammons stepped into the spotlight to form his own combo, playing blues-infused jazz. His version of "My Foolish Heart" (1950) was the first release on the fledgling Chess Records label. Gene Ammons formed his famous alliance with saxophonist Sonny Stitt in 1950, with whom he recorded the two-tenor classic "Blues Up and Down" that same year. For two years, the duo toured and recorded together before going off to front their own bands. Ammons' drug problems led to two jail sentences—from 1958-60 and 1962-69. After getting out of prison in 1969, Ammons' playing style changed a bit. He began incorporating some of the "frenzied" avant-garde style of playing that was in vogue at the time—but retained a funky rhythm section. Ammons continued to lead his own organ combos and soul-jazz groups until his death in 1974.

Musically speaking:

Influenced by Ben Webster, Lester Young, Coleman Hawkins, and Charlie Parker, Gene Ammons had a great impact on the world of R&B and jazz, influencing Stanley Turrentine, A.C. Reed, Houston Person, et al. Ammons combined Webster's tone and Young's scalar approach into an especially emotive ballad style. Ammons' harmonic conception reflected the modernism and sophistication of bebop with the soulful, gritty edge of the blues.

Here is a fine example of Ammons' behind-the-beat way of phrasing. Each chorus builds in intensity. Starting the solo in the middle register of the horn with a relaxed manner and lots of space affords lots of room to build. Each chorus gets a little busier and more harmonically complex, while the note selection steadily climbs up the horn, reaching a climax in the first two measures of section E. The solo begins mainly with chord tones, proceeding in measures A6-7 with a chromatic run up to the 3rd of the B♭ chord, anticipating it by a beat. In measures A9-10, the solo lands on a D♭—the ♭9 on a Cm7 and the ♭6 of F—but it works because it is the minor 3rd of the B♭ blues scale. Section B starts out with one of Ammons' pet licks (measures B1-2), sticks to chord tones in bars B3-7, then repeats the D♭ lick in measures B9-10. At section C, the solo begins to intensify. This time, a diminished lick is played on the last two beats of the four chord (measure C6), resolving into a B♭maj7 chord (measure C7). In the fourth chorus, harmonic variation is used with a scalar lick on the first measure of the IV chord, then an implied ♯IV diminished in measure D6. Each time something "out" is played, it is immediately followed by something "in." Measures D8-9 feature a nice bebop mixolydian lick that can be extracted and learned in every key. Ammons' style, while firmly rooted in the blues, has the harmonic sophistication of bebop. At measure E4, an A♭7(♭5) passing chord is played, resolving nicely back to B♭. Measures E6-12 are pure Charlie Parker influence.

Fig. 12

Gene Ammons Selected Discography

1950   *Blues Up and Down Vol. 1* – Prestige

1960   *Boss Tenor* – Prestige

1960   *Gene Ammons Story: Organ Combo* – Prestige

1961   *Boss Tenors: Straight Ahead from Chicago 1961* – Verve (with Sonny Stitt)

Jimmy Forrest fronting his band at the Pin-Up Room in St. Louis in 1948.
L–R: Clark Terry, trumpet; Charles Cotter, drums; Forrest, and Sykes Smith, trumpet.

JIMMY "NIGHT TRAIN" FORREST

(1920 – 1980)

Best known for his recording of "Night Train" which became an R&B standard, Jimmy Forrest was born and raised in St. Louis, Missouri. At age twelve, he joined his mother's band, Eva Forrest's Stompers. As a teenager in St. Louis, he played with early jazz piano legend Fate Marable, Eddie Johnson, and the Jeter-Pillars Orchestra. In the forties, Forrest hit the road, hooking up with Kansas City big band leader Jay McShann's Orchestra, then with Andy Kirk, and finally with Duke Ellington in 1949. The fifties found him back in St. Louis leading his own combo. In 1951, he recorded his classic "Night Train" (based on Ellington's tune "Happy Go Lucky Local"), which became one of the most recorded songs in the history of R&B. He became a popular performer on the R&B circuit and recorded several jazz-inflected R&B singles over the next few years, though none had the impact of "Night Train." From 1958 to 1963, Forrest collaborated with trumpet player Harry "Sweets" Edison, then joined the Count Basie Orchestra from 1973-78. (He was one of the few to play with both Ellington and Basie, two of the greatest and most influential big band leaders.) Forrest then co-led a group with trombonist Al Grey until his death in 1980.

Musically Speaking:

Jimmy "Night Train" Forrest was heavily influenced by Ben Webster and Coleman Hawkins, posessing a warm, reedy tone with a rich, full vibrato and a loping swing. He was able to master soulful simplicity as well as the complexities of modern jazz.

The following is an example of Forrest's bop-influenced blues style. Forrest brings out the sound of the chord changes by combining a blues scale approach that uses both a minor 3rd and a major 3rd with an arpeggiated approach. He not only outlines the basic changes, but often implies harmonic substitutions for flavor. His mastery of the double-time swing feel and his irregular grouping of notes mark this as a bebop rather than swing-era improvisation. Tightly structured, the first chorus is built off a Charlie Parker-inspired motif, followed by another Parker lick at measures A4 and A5 (à la "KC Blues"). The second Parker lick is extended to create a longer phrase (measure A6-7).

The second chorus begins with a new motif based off of the 7th. This motif, based on blue notes, heightens the emotional impact. At measure B6, an altered ♭9 arpeggio is employed, flowing right back into a blues scale lick. The final chorus begins with a recapitulation of the original theme based off the 7th—this time for greater emotional intensity. The solo climaxes at measure C5, where tension is built by stating an idea, then immediately playing the same line up a half step. The release occurs by moving back "inside" with an arpeggio based on chord tones.

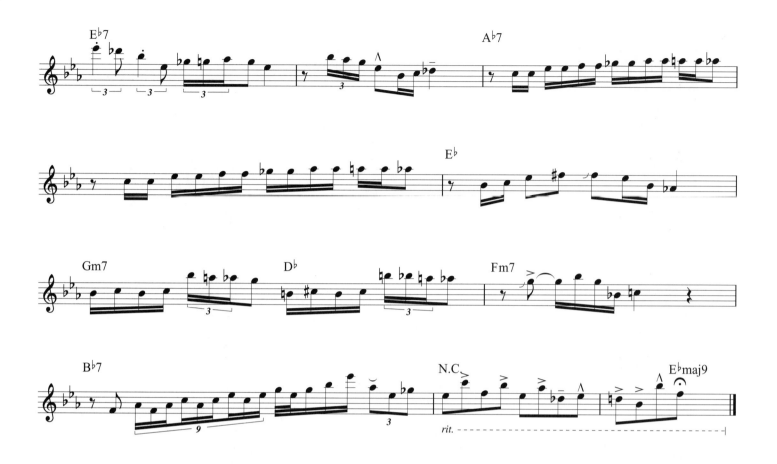

Jimmy "Night Train" Forrest Selected Discography

1951	*Night Train* – Delmark
1960	*Forrest Fire* – Prestige/Original Jazz
1961	*Out Of The Forrest* – Prestige/Original Jazz
1961	*Most Much!* – Prestige/Original Jazz

Eddie "Lockjaw" Davis in a publicity shot from the forties.
Hard swinging, blues-drenched solos were his trademark.

EDDIE "LOCKJAW" DAVIS

(1922 – 1986)

In the mold of Coleman Hawkins and Ben Webster, Eddie "Lockjaw" Davis' playing style was pure swing and blues. Raised in New York City, Davis was self-taught on the saxophone. His early years were spent hanging out and playing at the birthplace of bebop, Minton's Playhouse. He made a name for himself while playing in the sax sections of big bands lead by Cootie Williams, Lucky Millinder, and Andy Kirk.

Davis began his longstanding on-again, off-again association as featured soloist with the Count Basie Orchestra in 1952. He left the band in 1953, re-joined for part of '57, then again from 1964–73. From 1955-1960 (except for the brief period with the Basie Orchestra in '57), Davis teamed with organist Shirley Scott. Their series of "Cookbook" records stand as some of the earliest and most influential of the jazz organ/tenor genre (a style that became very popular in the early sixties).

Some of Davis' most memorable associations were his "tenor battles" with other sax players—Arnett Cobb, Sonny Stitt, and especially Johnny Griffin. Tenor battles had been taking place since the thirties, when the Basie Orchestra featured Lester Young and Herschel Evans. As "Lockjaw" explained to Pete Welding in Down Beat (June 22, 1961): "It's not really a battle at all. What we are presenting, side by side, are two different styles of playing tenor—a contrast, not a contest." Davis and Griffin were an ideal combination. Both played with lots of excitement, soaring technique, and a down-home blues feel. Playing off each other, they created an intense, high-voltage excitement.

After leaving the Basie Orchestra in 1973, Davis settled in Las Vegas. He recorded a series of albums for Pablo, including sessions with all-star Basie reunion groups. Davis remained active until his death in 1986.

Musically speaking:

Arguably one of the hardest players to imitate, Eddie "Lockjaw" Davis had an extremely distinctive, easily identifiable sound with his "jerky," swinging style and gruff, barking tone.

"Lockjaw" peppered his solos with a lot of harmonic spice. One of his favorite devices was the tritone substitution (measures A4 and B3-4). He would superimpose a chord an augmented 4th away. In this case, over the B♭7, he plays E major and uses it passing into the E♭7. This works because the B♭7 and the E7 share the same 3rd and 7th (D, G♯, or A♭). By playing a simple arpeggio on beats three and four, Davis would create an altered extension that resolves nicely into the IV chord. This harmonic device works best when you have root motion of a 4th.

To gain facility with this new concept, make up your own exercises and practice them with the track. In every chorus, over the last two beats of the fourth measure, create some kind of E major arpeggio to lead you into the E♭. Have fun experimenting, and remember to KEEP IT SIMPLE and select notes from the chord. Triads work best—if you were to use other notes derived from the chord scale, you would find it counterproductive. By altering the extension—say, a ♭9 on the E7 chord—you would have an F, and that would revert you back to chord tones from B♭.

Fig. 14

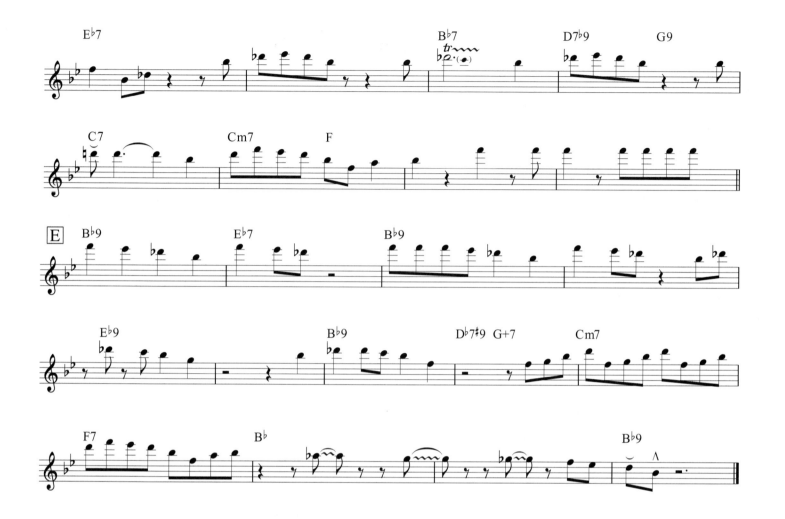

Eddie "Lockjaw" Davis Selected Discography

1958   *Eddie "Lockjaw" Davis Cookbook Vol. 1, 2, 3* (w/Shirley Scott) – Prestige

1959   *Very Saxy* (w/Buddy Tate, Arnett Cobb, and Coleman Hawkins) – Prestige

1960   *Trane Whistle* (w/Oliver Nelson) – Prestige

1961   *Live At Minton's* (w/Johnny Griffin) – Prestige

1969   *Jazz Fest Masters* (w/Count Basie) – Jazz Masters

WILLIS "GATOR" JACKSON

(1932 – 1987)

Willis "Gator" Jackson's full-throated tone and strong improvisational skills made him equally adept at R&B and jazz.

Willis Jackson played locally in his native Florida until joining former Duke Ellington trumpet player Cootie Williams' big band at age sixteen. Jackson was featured on Williams' 1948 hit, the honking R&B tune "Gator Tail" (from which he got his nickname). He began recording as a leader in 1950 but also continued to tour on and off with Williams until 1955. Jackson worked closely with Ruth Brown for eight years in the fifties (during the height of her career), playing on numerous sessions for Atlantic, backing her and others. He led his own organ combo and was responsible for discovering guitarist Pat Martino and organist Captain Jack McDuff. His extensive series of Prestige recordings (1959-64) made him a big attraction on the soul/jazz organ circuit. Jackson continued to tour steadily thru the seventies and eighties.

Musically speaking:

Willis "Gator" Jackson's style of playing was heavily influenced by Illinois Jacquet, incorporating equal parts jump-blues and classic organ soul/jazz with honking, hell-raising tenor solos. He had blazing, rapid-fire technique with a "voice" that was earthy, raucous, passionate, and aggressive.

This solo is based on a classic organ-combo sound that shows Jackson in a relaxed setting. It features the G minor blues scale, with a liberal use of the flat five to enhance the blues feel. Measures A1-7 are two-measure phrases based on the opening lick. Measure A8 is really the only time the solo veers away from the minor blues scale by outlining the B7–E7 chord changes. The second chorus turns up the heat, returning to the original blues scale but adding intensity until the solo climaxes at B10.

Looking very stylish in this photo from the 1950s,
"Gator" was equal parts jump-blues and soulful organ-combo jazz.

15 **Fig. 15**

Willis "Gator" Jackson Selected Discography

1959   *Please Mr. Jackson* – Original Jazz Classics

1960   *Together Again* – Prestige

1977   *Bar Wars* – Muse

Frank Driggs Collection

"Blowing Cool" in plaid and stripes, Stanley Turrentine's style
featured a large rich tone and searing blues solos.

STANLEY TURRENTINE

(1934 – 2000)

A soulful sax player equally adept at jazz, blues, and R&B, Pittsburgh native Stanley Turrentine grew up in a musical family: His mother played piano; his father played sax and taught him to play. (He showed him only one note per week, so he would focus on developing a "sound.") His brother Tommy was a professional trumpet player.

Stanley Turrentine's first professional gig was with guitarist Lowell Fulson's Blues Band (1950-51). Ray Charles was piano player in the band at the time. From 1953 to 1954, Turrentine worked with sax player Earl Bostic's R&B band, in which he replaced John Coltrane. He briefly worked with drummer Max Roach from 1959-60. Turrentine made his first album as a leader for Blue Note during that same period. In the early 1960s, he married organist Shirley Scott, and they played and recorded together over the next decade. The sixties also found him in the company of B3 master Jimmy Smith. Their classic organ recordings "Back at the Chicken Shack" and "Midnight Special" were from the same recording session on April 25, 1960. In the seventies, Turrentine crossed over into the pop field for a bit, making records for CTI. The jazz content slipped, but his playing remained strong, even though the basic format was mood music. Several of his CTI, Elektra, Fantasy, and Blue Note albums made the charts during the seventies and eighties.

Stanley Turrentine returned to his jazz roots in the eighties, recording again with Blue Note Records. He continued touring and recording until his death in September 2000.

Musically speaking:

Stanley Turrentine is primarily identified with the jazz organ combo sound. A strong swing player who was heavily influenced by Ben Webster and Don Byas, Turrentine's most identifiable characteristic is his big, rich, lush tone. His phrasing draws on both modern jazz and R&B. Turrentine had the technique to really burn on the uptempo tunes, but truly sounded his best on blues and ballads.

This demonstration of Turrentine's soul-jazz style is mainly based on the G minor pentatonic scale. Notice how the fourth measure of each chorus—the G7—is altered, and the relative ii–V is added for harmonic variety. In the first chorus, measures A6-10 insinuate a 12/8 feel. This builds tension, and when the release comes by going back to 4/4, it makes the groove cut a little deeper. In the second chorus (in measure B4), a G+7 is arpeggiated to give the altered sound. At measure B10, a tritone substitution (A-flat) on the third and fourth beats leads nicely into the G7 chord. This time measure C4 is altered by a $\sharp$9/$\flat$9 lick. Measures C7 and C8 outline the G7 chord followed by E7($\flat$9) leading to an A7 chord, then back to the blues by hitting the G minor blues scale to complete the solo. This piece is a good example of how one can build a solo using shape and the gradual evolution of ideas.

16 **Fig. 16**

Stanley Turrentine Selected Discography

1960   *Blue Hour* – Blue Note

1960   *Back At The Chicken Shack* (with Jimmy Smith) – Blue Note

1960   *Midnight Special* (with Jimmy Smith) – Blue Note

1963   *Prayer Meetin'* (with Jimmy Smith) – Blue Note

1970   *Sugar* – CTI

1984   *Straight Ahead* – Blue Note

Sonny Stitt blowing a stinging sax solo at the Bee Hive in Chicago, 1950.

SONNY STITT

(1924 – 1982)

Born Edward Stitt in Boston, Sonny Stitt grew up in Saginaw, Michigan surrounded by music. His father was a music teacher; his mother played piano and organ. Sonny's brother Clifford was a concert pianist. At age seven, Sonny started playing piano, later switching to clarinet then alto sax.

Sonny Stitt made his recording debut with Tiny Bradshaw in the early forties. His early influences were Johnny Hodges and Benny Carter. He joined Billy Eckstine's revolutionary bebop-based big band in 1945, part of a sax section that also included Dexter Gordon and Gene Ammons. In this setting, Stitt found a musical situation conducive to his advanced style of playing. 1946 found him working on and off with Eckstine, but he was also a member of the first short-lived Dizzy Gillespie big band, recording with Gillespie in May of that year.

After a prison term for a drug bust, Stitt moved to New York City in 1949 and found bebop waning; Miles Davis was already "blowing cool." Stitt was growing tired of always being cast in the Charlie Parker mold and he found that, by switching to tenor, he could distance himself from comparisons to Bird. (He didn't go back to the alto until after Bird's death in 1955.) His sound on tenor became markedly more individual—influenced by Lester Young, Don Byas, and his old bandmate Dexter Gordon. Stitt first recorded on tenor for trombonist J.J. Johnson's session in 1949. He also did several albums with his own combo for Prestige, Argo, and Verve during the fifties. For a brief period in 1960, Stitt joined Miles Davis—replacing John Coltrane. That was, however, short-lived; Miles felt that Stitt's solos were too bebop-based for his modal excursions of the time. Following Miles, Stitt played and recorded with many different organ combos—Don Patterson and Brother Jack McDuff, among others. Stitt also co-led a group with Gene Ammons for some classic two-tenor "battles."

In 1971, Stitt joined the all-star aggregation "Giants Of Jazz," a band that included Gillespie, Thelonious Monk, Kai Winding, Art Blakey, and Al McKibbon. He continued to play and record up until his death in 1982.

Musically speaking:

A great ballad and blues player, Sonny Stitt's playing was driven by a forceful rhythmic sense, precise articulation, and blazing technique. Everything he played had a touch of bebop to it. His playing was characterized by a syncopated sense of rhythm, melodies made up primarily of eighth notes, chromatic approaches to chord tones, and chords with altered 5ths and 9ths. With his reedy tone and light touch, Stitt's music was always strong and immediate.

This 12-Bar uptempo blues is a good example of Stitt's style, incorporating long flowing lines and implying harmonic substitutions and chord alterations. Section G employs an example of rhythmic displacement—taking a three-note pattern (G–F♯–D) and repeating it, constantly displacing where the notes fall within the measure (measures G1-5). The pattern is continued through the IV chord, changing the F-sharp to F natural to fit the chord change. Tension is built until the release at measure G6, coming out of the pattern with a blues lick followed by a chromatic approach to the flat V of the F♯m7(♭5) chord. Section H uses the same rhythmic displacement device, this time using a six-note pattern (D–F♯–G–A– G–F♯). Section J is a "kick" chorus similar to what you would hear in a big-band arrangement. Section K is another favorite device of Stitt's—the long outro vamp at the end of a song. Using a repeated four-measure vamp comprised of a ii–V pattern (Em7–A7–F♯m7–B7), this section starts out sparse and builds to a climax by the use of repeated figures, gradually incorporating longer lines.

If you have difficulty at first playing at this tempo, try slowing it down, placing the metronome on beats 2 and 4, then gradually increasing the tempo.

17 Fig. 17

Sonny Stitt Selected Discography

1949   *Sonny Stitt with Bud Powell & J.J. Johnson* – Prestige

1961   *Boss Tenors (w/Gene Ammons)* – Verve

1962   *Stitt meets Brother Jack (w/Jack McDuff)* – Prestige

????   *Soul Classics 1962-1972* – Prestige

1972   *Tune-Up* – Muse

Photo by Paul Natkin

*Sonny Rollins, "lost in the muse" with the look of pure joy on his face,
blowing one of his exuberant sax solos.*

SONNY ROLLINS

(1930 –)

Perhaps the most enigmatic figure jazz has known, Sonny Rollins has been a commanding presence since the fifties. Theodore Rollins grew up in the Sugar Hill section of Harlem. He began studying music on piano and switched to sax by age eleven. Coleman Hawkins lived in his neighborhood and was an early influence on Rollins.

At age nineteen, Sonny Rollins made his recording debut with singer Babs Gonzales. For the next six years, he recorded as a sideman with such jazz luminaries as J.J. Johnson, Bud Powell, Thelonious Monk, and Miles Davis (who paired him up with a tenor-playing Charlie Parker in 1955). Rollins' reputation began to grow from his outstanding work in the Clifford Brown/Max Roach quintet. When that group disbanded due to Brown's untimely death, Rollins headed out on his own.

Rollins' early recordings displayed a talented player in the style of Dexter Gordon. This manner of playing combined the robust tone of Coleman Hawkins (sans vibrato) with the rhythmic and asymmetrical phrasing of Lester Young. By 1956, Rollins had discovered his own voice and released his landmark recording *Saxophone Colossus*. At age twenty-seven, his playing demonstrated a sense of maturity. He displayed a sardonic wit and an ability to organize his ideas in such a fashion that his improvisational style became known as "thematic improvisation." He would get inside of an idea or theme, cull from it, distill its essence, and use it for a serious of variations—often forsaking the chord changes to keep the embellishments going. In 1957, Rollins decided to record an album (*Way Out West*) with just bass and drums (eliminating the piano)—an idea he had experimented with before, but not for an entire recording. This allowed him to play fragments of themes in even more harmonic variations without being boxed in by a chordal instrument. Still using the trio format, Rollins released *Freedom Suite* in 1958, in which he addressed racial and artistic freedom.

By 1959, not yet thirty, Rollins took the first of his self-imposed sabbaticals. He used this time to reinvent himself, spending many nights practicing on NYC's Williamsburg Bridge. Rollins developed a new tone—warmer and huskier—and formulated his "system of orchestration," a new way of arranging his thematic approach. After a two-year break, he returned to the studio, signing a lucrative contract to record six albums for RCA. The first of these is called (naturally) *The Bridge*. All six of the RCA recordings, although not commercially successful, were masterful and groundbreaking—covering the spectrum of jazz from hard bop to latin and even including a foray into Ornette Coleman-inspired free jazz.

In 1967, Rollins took another self-imposed exile and did not enter a recording studio for five years. This time, when he returned, he had again reinvented himself, using a more pentatonic-modal approach with a broader, edgier tone.

When Sonny Rollins is at his best, he is completely vulnerable and exposes himself more than almost any other musician. He leaves an unparalleled legacy of monumental improvisations. Rollins, whose live performances continue to be the stuff that legends are made of, is still very active today.

Musically speaking:

While not generally considered a blues player (but rather a major stylistic modernist), Sonny Rollins takes a unique approach to the blues that deserves attention. Arguably the greatest living saxophonist, with his huge, edgy, resonant tone, speech-like phrasing, harmonic approach, and thematic style of improvisation, Rollins defies categorization.

This 12-bar blues is based on the Lydian dominant scale. This scale emphasizes the sharp 11th of the chord. To find the appropriate notes, build an augmented major 7 chord on the ♭7 of each chord of the progression (for a C7 chord: B-flat–D–F♯–A; for a F7 chord: E-flat–G–B–D; etc.)

Another way to find the notes is to play the C Lydian dominant scale (C–D–E–F♯–G–A–B♭—a Mixolydian scale with a raised 4th degree).

The opening three notes serve as the principal motif for the solo (measures A1-8, A12-B1, B8-11). The endless variations of this simple motif that he spontaneously creates are the essence of his improvisational style. Rollins likes to use double-time bebop licks to connect his ideas and build excitement (measures A9-11, B12-C1, D5-9). At measures D10-11, the solo temporarily deviates from the Lydian dominant scale and uses a Charlie Parker-inspired lick.

To familiarize yourself with this new sound, first practice the augmented major 7 arpeggio with the track, building it off of the seventh degree of the chord. Then play the corresponding Lydian dominant scales to get the sound in your head. It may sound strange at first, but it's important to first train your ear to this new sound in order for it to come out in your playing.

18 Fig. 18

Sonny Rollins Selected Discography

1956   *Saxophone Colossus* – Original Jazz Classics

1957   *Way Out West* – Original Jazz Classics

1957   *Night At The Village Vanguard Vols. I & II (Live)* – Blue Note

1962   *The Bridge* – Bluebird/RCA

1972   *Sonny Rollins' Next Album* – Milestone

BIBLIOGRAPHY

BOOKS

Bailey, Derek: *Improvisation: Its Nature & Practice In Music* – Da Capo Press.

Berry, Jason, Jonathan Foose, and Tad Jones:
  Up From the Cradle of Jazz: New Orleans Music Since WWII – University of Georgia Press.

Coker, Jerry: *Listening to Jazz* – Prentice Hall.

Dance, Stanley: *The World of Count Basie* – DaCapo Press.

Erlewine, Michael and Scott Bultman, eds.: *All Music Guide* – Miller Freeman Books.

Erlewine, Michael and Vladimir Bogdaov, Chris Woodstra, Cub Koda, eds.:
  All Music Guide to the Blues – Miller Freeman Books.

Giddins, Gary: *Visions Of Jazz: The First Century* – Oxford Press.

Gitler, Ira: *Swing to Bop* – Oxford University Press.

Shaw, Arnold Honkers & Shouters: *The Golden Years of Rhythm & Blues* – Collier Books.

Rucker, Leland: ed. *Music Hound Blues: The Essential Guide* – Visible Ink.

Santelli, Robert: *The Big Book of the Blues: A Biographical Encyclopedia* – Penguin.

Williams, Martin: *The Jazz Tradition* – Oxford Press.

Yanow, Scott: *Swing* – Miller Freeman Books.

ARTICLES

Bonner, Brett: "Eddie Shaw." *Living Blues*, November/December 1995.

Danchin, Sebastian: "A. C. Reed." *Living Blues*, November/December 1995.

Hildebrand, Lee: "Don't Cry No More: The Life & Death of an East Bay Blues Master."
  Blue Access, Fall 2000.

Kunian, David: "Master of Louisiana Music – Lee Allen." *Offbeat*, December 2000.

Nisenson, Eric: "Sonny Rollins Is in the House." *JazzOne*, April 1999.

ALBUM NOTES

Crouch, Stanley: *Illinois Jacquet: Banned in Boston* – CBS Records 1989.

Gitler, Ira: *Griff & Lock* – Jazzland 1960.

Porter, Bob: *Atlantic Honkers: A Rhythm & Blues Anthology* – Atlantic 1986.

Porter, Bob: *Jacquet's Got It* – Atlantic 1988.

Bell, Bob: *Rock On Roll: The Best of Red Prysock* – Avi 1996.

ABOUT THE AUTHOR

Two-time (2000 and 1999) Nashville Music Awards nominee for "Miscellaneous Wind Instrumentalist of the Year," saxophonist DENNIS TAYLOR (tenor, alto, soprano, and baritone) has been playing the saxophone for more than twenty-five years, performing professionally for the last twenty. He's performed and toured with a wide variety of artists including Clarence "Gatemouth" Brown, Buckwheat Zydeco, Duke Robillard, Shelby Lynne, Eddy "The Chief" Clearwater, Robert Jr. Lockwood, "Mighty" Sam McClain, Sam Moore (Sam & Dave), the Excello Legends (Earl Gaines and Roscoe Shelton), Dan Penn, Jay McShann, and John Hammond. Dennis has played on four Grammy-nominated albums. He has appeared on "Austin City Limits," "The Road," "Country Music Hall of Fame 25th Anniversary Celebration," "Texas Connection," "ABC in Concert Country," "American Music Shop," and "Music City Tonight."

Raised in the Northeast Kingdom of Vermont, Dennis began studying the saxophone at age nine. After graduating high school, he attended Berklee College of Music. Following that, he became an adjunct professor of music, teaching both private sax lessons and improvisational workshops, at Johnson State College, Johnson, VT. In addition, he performed regularly with various local Vermont jazz and R&B bands. In 1980, he moved to New Orleans, where he played many diverse musical styles—from dixieland and salsa to New Orleans R&B and the deep soul music of "Mighty" Sam McClain. In 1983, he joined up with Grammy-award winning multi-instrumentalist Clarence "Gatemouth" Brown, playing everything from blues shuffles to zydeco, Count Basie instrumentals, country fiddle breakdowns, calypso numbers, and pop standards. In late 1985, after two years of touring and recording with "Gatemouth" Brown, Dennis moved to Boston. In October 1987, he joined Island Records recording artist Buckwheat Zydeco and continued to tour and record with the band (including an eight-week U.S. and UK tour with Eric Clapton, several dates with U2 and Los Lobos, and tours to Australia and Japan) until January 1991.

In December 1989, Dennis relocated to Nashville. In the mid-nineties, he toured with Shelby Lynne, Kenny Rogers, Sam Moore, and the Excello Legends. From October 1997 to November 1999, Dennis toured with Duke Robillard. (During that time, Robillard's band was nominated for the W.C. Handy Award "Blues Band of the Year.") Splitting his time between periodic tours with Eddy "The Chief" Clearwater and "Gatemouth" Brown, Dennis continues to do session work and teach while freelancing at home in Nashville. This is his first book for Hal Leonard Corporation.

ACKNOWLEDGMENTS

To Dave Rubin, who helped make this possible; Frank-John Hadley, Michael Gray (You're the "Prez"), Nadine "Bloodhound" Cohodas, who helped me dig up the facts; Shelton Clark for planting the seed; Steve Herrman for his tremendous musicality; Fred James (producer, guitar player, general support and source material), and all the soulful players: Bob Kommersmith (bass), Bryan Owings (drums), Phil Rugh (keyboards); Jeff Kirk (sax guru); Clarence "Gatemouth" Brown, Stanley "Buckwheat Zydeco" Dural, Jr., Robert Jr. Lockwood, and Duke Robillard for the great experience of learning first hand by their side the various shades of the blues; my parents Lois and Ad Taylor for their constant support and encouragement , and especially my wife Karen Leipziger who has shown me that the only limits we have are self-imposed.

I dedicate this book to Karen for her love and support (and editing). Her belief in me has been unswerving.

RECORDING CREDITS

Fred James, co-producer/guitar player

Joe Funderburk, recording and mixing engineer

Bob Kommersmith, bass

Bryan Owings, drums

Phil Rugh, keyboards

Dennis Taylor, tenor saxophone

Recorded at Three Little Pigs Studio, Nashville, TN February 2001

ARTIST TRANSCRIPTIONS®

Artist Transcriptions are authentic, note-for-note transcriptions of the hottest artists in jazz, pop, and rock today. These outstanding, accurate arrangements are in an easy-to-read format which includes all essential lines. Artist Transcriptions can be used to perform, sequence or reference.

GUITAR & BASS

The Guitar Style of George Benson
00660113......................................$14.95

The Guitar Book of Pierre Bensusan
00699072......................................$19.95

Ron Carter – Acoustic Bass
00672331......................................$16.95

Charley Christian –
The Art of Jazz Guitar
00026704....................................... $9.95

Stanley Clarke Collection
00672307......................................$19.95

Al Di Meola – Cielo E Terra
00604041......................................$14.95

Al Di Meola –
Friday Night in San Francisco
00660115......................................$14.95

Al Di Meola – Music, Words, Pictures
00604043......................................$14.95

Kevin Eubanks Guitar Collection
00672319......................................$19.95

The Jazz Style of Tal Farlow
00673245......................................$19.95

Bela Fleck and the Flecktones
00672359 Melody/Lyrics/Chords....$16.95

David Friesen – Years Through Time
00673253......................................$14.95

Best Of Frank Gambale
00672336......................................$22.95

Jim Hall – Jazz Guitar Environments
00699389 Book/CD $19.95

Jim Hall – Exploring Jazz Guitar
00699306......................................$17.95

Scott Henderson Guitar Book
00699330......................................$19.95

Allan Holdsworth –
Reaching for the Uncommon Chord
00604049......................................$14.95

Leo Kottke – Eight Songs
00699215......................................$14.95

Wes Montgomery – Guitar Transcriptions
00675536......................................$17.95

Joe Pass Collection
00672353......................................$18.95

John Patitucci
00673216......................................$14.95

Django Reinhardt Anthology
00027083......................................$14.95

The Genius of Django Reinhardt
00026711......................................$10.95

Django Reinhardt – A Treasury of Songs
00026715......................................$12.95

Great Rockabilly Guitar Solos
00692820......................................$14.95

Johnny Smith Guitar Solos
00672374......................................$16.95

Mike Stern Guitar Book
00673224......................................$16.95

Mark Whitfield
00672320......................................$19.95

Jack Wilkins – Windows
00673249......................................$14.95

Gary Willis Collection
00672337......................................$19.95

CLARINET

Buddy De Franco Collection
00672423......................................$19.95

TROMBONE

J.J. Johnson Collection
00672332......................................$19.95

TRUMPET

The Chet Baker Collection
00672435......................................$19.95

Randy Brecker
00673234......................................$14.95

The Brecker Brothers...
And All Their Jazz
00672351......................................$19.95

Best of the Brecker Brothers
00672447......................................$19.95

Miles Davis – Originals
00672448......................................$19.95

FLUTE

James Newton – Improvising Flute
00660108......................................$14.95

The Lew Tabackin Collection
00672455......................................$19.95

Miles Davis – Standards Vol. 1
00672450......................................$19.95

The Dizzy Gillespie Collection
00672479......................................$19.95

Freddie Hubbard
00673214......................................$14.95

Tom Harrell Jazz Trumpet
00672382......................................$19.95

Jazz Trumpet Solos
00672363......................................$9.95

PIANO & KEYBOARD

Monty Alexander Collection
00672338......................................$19.95

Kenny Barron Collection
00672318......................................$22.95

Warren Bernhardt Collection
00672364......................................$19.95

Cyrus Chesnut Collection
00672439......................................$19.95

Billy Childs Collection
00673242......................................$19.95

Chick Corea – Elektric Band
00603126......................................$15.95

Chick Corea – Paint the World
00672300......................................$12.95

Bill Evans Collection
00672365......................................$19.95

Benny Green Collection
00672329......................................$19.95

Herbie Hancock Collection
00672419......................................$19.95

Gene Harris Collection
00672446......................................$19.95

Ahmad Jamal Collection
00672322......................................$22.95

Jazz Master Classics for Piano
00672354......................................$14.95

Thelonious Monk – Intermediate
Piano Solos
00672392......................................$14.95

Jelly Roll Morton – The Piano Rolls
00672433......................................$12.95

Michel Petrucciani
00673226......................................$17.95

Bud Powell Classics
00672371......................................$19.95

André Previn Collection
00672437......................................$19.95

Horace Silver Collection
00672303......................................$19.95

Art Tatum Collection
00672316......................................$22.95

Art Tatum Solo Book
00672355......................................$19.95

Billy Taylor Collection
00672357......................................$24.95

McCoy Tyner
00673215......................................$16.95

Cedar Walton Collection
00672321......................................$19.95

SAXOPHONE

Julian "Cannonball" Adderly Collection
00673244......................................$18.95

Michael Brecker
00673237......................................$19.95

Michael Brecker Collection
00672429......................................$19.95

The Brecker Brothers...
And All Their Jazz
00672351......................................$19.95

Best of the Brecker Brothers
00672447......................................$19.95

Benny Carter Plays Standards
00672315......................................$22.95

Benny Carter Collection
00672314......................................$22.95

James Carter Collection
00672394......................................$19.95

John Coltrane – Giant Steps
00672349......................................$19.95

John Coltrane Solos
00673233......................................$22.95

Paul Desmond Collection
00672328......................................$19.95

Paul Desmond – Standard Time
00672454......................................$19.95

Stan Getz
00699375......................................$18.95

Stan Getz – Bossa Novas
00672377......................................$19.95

Stan Getz – Standards
00672375......................................$17.95

Great Tenor Sax Solos
00673254......................................$18.95

Joe Henderson – Selections from
"Lush Life" & "So Near So Far"
00673252......................................$19.95

Best of Joe Henderson
00672330......................................$22.95

Jazz Master Classics for Tenor Sax
00672350......................................$18.95

Best Of Kenny G
00673239......................................$19.95

Kenny G – Breathless
00673229......................................$19.95

Kenny G – Classics in the Key of G
00672462......................................$19.95

Kenny G – The Moment
00672373......................................$19.95

Joe Lovano Collection
00672326......................................$19.95

James Moody Collection – Sax and Flute
00672372......................................$19.95

The Frank Morgan Collection
00672416......................................$19.95

The Art Pepper Collection
00672301......................................$19.95

Sonny Rollins Collection
00672444......................................$19.95

David Sanborn Collection
00675000......................................$16.95

The Lew Tabackin Collection
00672455......................................$19.95

Stanley Turrentine Collection
00672334......................................$19.95

Ernie Watts Saxophone Collection
00673256......................................$18.95

FOR MORE INFORMATION, SEE YOUR LOCAL MUSIC DEALER,
OR WRITE TO:

HAL•LEONARD®
CORPORATION
7777 W. BLUEMOUND RD. P.O. BOX 13819 MILWAUKEE, WI 53213

Visit our web site for a complete listing of our titles with songlists.
www.halleonard.com